HYEM

Robyn Bolam, freelance poet, editor and reviewer, was born in Newcastle, grew up in Northumberland and now lives in Hampshire. She is Emeritus Professor at St Mary's University, a former Royal Literary Fund Fellow at Southampton University and RLF Lector on the Isle of Wight. In 2016-17, she led the community-based, combined arts Ferry Tales Project which was supported using public funding by the National Lottery through Arts Council England. She has published four collections with Bloodaxe: *The Peepshow Girl* (1989), *Raiding the Borders* (1996), *New Wings: Poems 1997-2007* (2007), a Poetry Book Society Recommendation, and *Hyem* (2017). She is the editor of *Eliza's Babes: four centuries of women's poetry in English, 1500-1900* (Bloodaxe Books, 2005), and five seventeenth-century plays. Other works include a monograph on Shakespeare and his contemporaries and essays on drama and poetry from the Renaissance to the present day.

In 1981, she received an Eric Gregory Award and won first prize in the Cheltenham Festival Poetry Competition. Her libretto for the opera *Beyond Men and Dreams* (composer Bennett Hogg) was performed by the Royal Opera House Garden Venture in 1991. She was awarded a Hawthornden International Fellowship in 1993, held a British Council writing residency at the University of Stockholm in 1998 and was Writer in Residence at the University of Reading, 2010-11, and at Southampton University's Tony Davies High Voltage Laboratory in 2012, the inaugural year of the Litmus Project. She has given readings of her poetry in Britain, Portugal, Sweden, Romania, USA and Japan.

www.robynbolam.com

ROBYN BOLAM

HYEM

BLOODAXE BOOKS

ISBN: 978 1 78037 394 2

First published 2017 by
Bloodaxe Books Ltd,
Eastburn,
South Park,
Hexham,
Northumberland NE46 1BS.

www.bloodaxebooks.com
For further information about Bloodaxe titles
please visit our website or write to
the above address for a catalogue.

Supported using public funding by
ARTS COUNCIL
ENGLAND

Cover design: Neil Astley & Pamela Robertson-Pearce.

Printed in Great Britain by Bell & Bain Limited, Glasgow, Scotland, on
acid-free paper sourced from mills with FSC chain of custody certification.

Hyem, yem, hame, home.
Rest safely;
be always welcome.

ACKNOWLEDGEMENTS

Acknowledgements are due to the editors of the following publications in which some of these poems, or versions of them, first appeared: *A Mutual Friend: Poems for Charles Dickens* (Two Rivers Press with the English Association, 2012), *Beached here at random by mysterious forces* (School of English, University of Kent, 2015), *Feeling the Pressure: Poetry and science of climate change* (British Council, 2008), *Heart Shoots* (Macmillan Cancer Support/Indigo Dreams, 2013), *London Magazine* (August/September 2009), *London Rivers 2* (Paekakariki Press, 2017), *Nothing like concrete* (University of Reading, 2011), *Poetry Review* 103:4 (Winter 2013), *Riptide* issue 9 (2013), Poetry Salzburg Review 13 (Spring 2008), *The New Forester* (2013), and *Two Thirds North* (Stockholm University & Cinnamon Press, 2016).

'Winter Solstice at the High Voltage Laboratory' and 'Jacob's Ladder' began as part of the Litmus Project, in association with the Director of the University of Southampton's High Voltage Laboratory, Professor Paul Lewin, and his research team. The project was set up by Frances Clarke in collaboration with Professor Peter Middleton and Dr Will May from the Department of English: www.litmusprojectsouthampton.com

I am grateful to present and past members of the Spring Poets' Poetry Workshop at Havant who continue to provide an enthusiastic sounding board as well as much friendship, and to the Royal Literary Fund for years of encouragement and support.

CONTENTS

WHERE HOME STARTED

Where Home Started

I used to cross the Tyne to school. Days raced
on a rattling, crowded bus, hands gripping
fingered chrome, knees braced against straining seats.
Once, reading *The Return of the Native*
in too-dull light – the Tyne below Scotswood,
dark and silent under the bus's roar –
wheels left the road and we slipped down a bank
to halt feet away from lapping water.
Cocooned in gabardine, I was handed
out through the upturned emergency door,
clutching my satchel.

Then, while the shipyard lads lit cigarettes,
we huddled, stamping, at the river's edge,
watched the steady lights of a pilot boat
speed uptide, bringing in cargo too big
to go it alone, and a police launch
on its routine patrol. Still shivering
in near-dark, I could smell the river tang,
sense submerged lives and deaths, feel a current
pull, inside me, as it does whenever
I think of home. Whatever depths there were,
we never reached them.

Changing Sequence

When a bearded ghost peering into your cot, or your mother
mashing a mouse with a poker against the stone kitchen floor
are your earliest memories, you switch chronology, prefer
to recall clean, raw sawdust clinging to the overalls
your father wore, the jingling of their metal clasps
as he threw back the straps and pulled you onto his toes
to dance on the hearthrug, hugging his knees. Perhaps
I'll go on doing it – juggling memories to bury those
I can't change or lose, but would rather not keep –
so my father will stay a fit, working man, swinging his child
onto his chest in the firelight while she tries not to succumb to sleep
and, at the riverside, it's summer, my mother drawing her dark head to mine
as we find ditches of marsh marigolds, hedgerows of purple vetch, to press
between these pages that smell both dead and fresh.

World-stretching

is something that happens in the dark of growing up.
Your small sphere, like a snub shoot, takes root.
The size of a cot, with its borders of blankets,
its bars, new tropics, your world grows
and the open sea of lino breaks out the bedroom door,
swells to an ocean of voices.

Soon your world has swallowed the whole house and garden,
is big enough to hold the road to school,
expands to Miss Hepple's class, a sand-pit,
and the bluebell wood you see through the window
while she reads stories about dying elephants
and Lord Nithsdale's daring escape in a dress
from a prison that might have killed him.

It runs to the cornfield behind the wood,
where an old man (who never molests you)
sleeps on summer nights – and the quarry
to which you ride your bike, without a helmet,
along the main road – and the park, where you
hang upside down, swinging from bent knees,
your hair sweeping jagged rocks
a foot or so beneath.
                            It reaches south
to the tadpole burn you fall into
with three friends on a chill spring day
and as far north as the Tyne you are told
not to wade in because the deep holes
dredged for gravel can suck you down forever
and you might die before your world stretched
out of the valley, or you could say
that you were ten.

Basil Bunting's Shadow

Whooom. I wake.
Whoom, whoom. In bed
I love the plaintive bass of horns at sea.
Sailors' extended voices
warning, warning, as day
rises through fog.

Safe and warm on land,
I pray no ill befalls the vessels'
close community. Though invisible
to one another, let them pass uneventfully
in these southern waters that he sailed
and I sail now.

In a room cold as a bell,
the see-saw horn of the first train
roused my young self from sleep before
early-morning workers, rattling in carriages,
stop-started at Prudhoe Station
for Newcastle Central.

The faces, on the train from Carlisle
carrying me to my new school, are gone.
Yet I have kept the signal box, fire-warmed
waiting-room, the station master's chickens
and my favourite bridge, half-moon,
single span, its wrought-iron arches

embracing bursts of green as wheels
rail-hugged through them to cross
the Tyne at Wylam, where he caught his train
to work at the *Chronicle*, scribbling *Briggflatts*
to the same rhythm I finished my homework.
It drowned out the river's elegies

for the ruined castle that Turner
thought worthy of a watercolour
before trees screened it between houses and factory.
Something was being mourned
long before I travelled with my teenage love, now lost,
long before these more than fifty years passed.

Something was always being mourned
by the wind from the north that scoured
the engineering works and shipyards.
I'm sure he heard it too. We never met
but, in the Newcastle early-morning rush,
perhaps our shadows touched uneventfully.

In Praise of Windows

(J.G. Windows, est. 1908, Central Arcade, Newcastle upon Tyne)

If keeping a dream meant that, one day, it came true,
I would live in this shop, learn the secrets of saxophones,
the tricks of trombones, the triumphs of trumpets,
how to charm a horn and cajole a cornet, make a flute take flight.

I'd practise in a never-ending cycle until I could play an orchestra,
or at least caress keys, finger strings, experiment with chords,
stroke the plush, crushed velour of cases, crawl inside the larger ones to sleep
pillowed on harmonies, and wake refreshed – like the never-dead, never-to-die.

The piccolo player upstairs can teach me.
We'll work through the sheet music, alternating with my favourite CDs,
listening, learning – from strings to brass to drums – and when we've done
we'll invite the buskers in with fiddle and ukulele – and dance a ceilidh.

Song for Voices

My mother's voice sings
inside mine, a birthplace song:
two counties duet.

Twice Removed

It took a hundred years to establish the name
of my grandfather's family in Orkney;
they travelled further north from the pit that claimed him,
to fish open sea under colder skies.

My grandmother's family may have reached Shetland earlier,
yet she stayed in County Durham to be a miner's wife,
both strands of ancestors lost among the islands
in salt-wind, lobster creels, thrift springing underfoot.

He was a tall man cramped, crawling through creaking shafts,
hot, black dust in nose and throat, eyes darting like trapped birds.
A bonxie takes off into my hair; its chick, soft brown down
on the grass by my feet. That old woman on her knees grubbing for tatties

may know the ones I seek – or the farmer, replacing thirty years
of fencing, who won't be doing it again. Everyone,
from puffins in precipitous crevices to the girl creating
co-operative crafts, moves constantly: sea to burrow,

fish to beaks, laptop to needle and rough-weave,
attaching stones from the beach. Out there, distant genetic links,
with dark hair and widows' peaks, turn calm eyes toward the haaf,
the clean cold freshening as the haar creeps.

Where are you from?

The locum held my arm gently, wrapped a cuff around it
and squeezed in air. 'Just round the corner,' I told him.
It was London. 'No, originally – where are you from?'
'Northumberland,' I said. 'But before you came to this country?'
'I was born in the north of England.' Why did this matter?
He apologised profusely. 'I'm so sorry; I thought you were like me.'

My blood group is more common in India; my hair and skin could
place me elsewhere. It's a mistake doctors had made before but,
unlike then, I felt sad at disappointing him. He might have been
happy to find we came from the same city or village. Go back
far enough and who knows? Perhaps we all have hidden links.
He didn't ask why my blood pressure was lower than usual.

'Where are you from?' It's the question at every border they reach
after walking miles in the rain, the heat. To say, 'Syria' might
take them through, though often, now, they are refused wherever
they've come from – Syria, Afghanistan, India, Nigeria, Pakistan.
When someone runs from war, danger, lack of food – perhaps,
just wants to thrive – where are the questions we need to ask?

Uisce Beatha

(in memory of Seamus Heaney,
13 April 1939 – 30 August 2013)

Like the brand of whisky he once mentioned,
he was unslick, anti-pretentious – a good malt:
rich, warming, with notes of moss, sky and honey,
a whiff of peat bog and organic matter, baled hay
and fermenting blackberries distilled in his flavour.

It was a farmer's whisky, reminiscent
of his rural roots, once hidden
as barrels marked for the sheep.
A self-deprecating drink, its connections
were rustic English and Scottish, not Irish.
He applauded the best, wherever it came from.

We're raising a glass to him now – sadly,
fondly, in praise and thanks for a man apart
and yet very much with us, raised under thatch.
He celebrated that, in word and sound, *uisce* and whiskey
coincide with water, the vital answer to all thirst.
Missing his generous spirit, we will savour his words,
roll them on our tongues year on year, mindful
of their potency, of his welcoming blackbird waiting.

Solent Song: Thursday 18th September 2014

I sailed across on Light, am returning on Sky,
overtaken by Sun. This is the land you can spy
from the high forest heath; these are the distant hills
over horses and heather, blue-washed, with wispy cirrus
presaging a new front above pale corn, green,
then grey, the white town trimmed with sails.

This is the land stretching along the Solent,
playing stand-off with the salt marsh to which it
was joined in the days when crocodiles swam
in its swamps. This is the land, once the far bank
of Solent River, facing lagoons and tracks leading
to a creek where sails float over fields, lanes sloe-laden.

I love this short voyage, half the hour-crossing to Arran,
sun on the water, a peaceful sky, harmonious chatter
floating over our broad wake, the marbled waves.
These hills hold your eyes in their own ways
even though, compared to Goat Fell, they are
the gentlest of mounds. How much better could it be

on the day part of my family made a choice:
to live in a separated country, or to stay attached right down
to this island but keep playing the stand-off game?

ELUSIVE NEIGHBOURS

Lost communities of Llanfaes

Bluebells stake rootholds in waves of wild garlic
then make a run for it across the wood, below
a canopy of new leaves, dizzily shifting squirrels
into hiding. Tufted ears twitch, rotate to our footfall.

It's too early for fruit, seeds and nuts – no
green acorns, a culled grey cousins' favourite –
but somewhere they nurture kittens in moss and grass,
dreys vibrating as multiple toes and fingers flex.

They are the winners, preferred, protected, who
might, if they wished, swim the straits at low tide,
ride a train to the mainland, swing over a bridge or,
with their double-jointed ankles, climb down head-first.

But we know they are here, holding up in hundreds,
despite road-kill. As we leave the wood, their rosehip,
carrot, crab-apple fur will wink in the sun behind us,
feather-boa tails wiggling a champions' wave.

Troglodytes Troglodytes

Doubly prehistoric,
you sound like
a small renaissance,
your voice, a cave echo,
bigger than
you are –

as if, once,
bird filled the size
of a song that ripples now
to a wheezy churr.
A tail tips up and I
see leaves stir.

Later, when
you're drenched
in a smothered bed,
the chestnut flash
of your barred back
hops as you hunt.

Tiniest, cockiest,
your feather charms
against disaster.
You belong
to the Old World.
Every night
I try to imagine

where the hens rest
when you are hiding,
how whole broods have flown
their hedges and gardens
to squeeze wings
beside you –

how ninety of you huddle
in one nest, press
feathers together
to wrench out winter,
renounce it to grow
bigger than cold.

Murmuration

Startled, we hear their favoured tree
before noticing how dark it is with wings,
how branches shake out the last November light.
Excitement skims across allotments
from their eager chattering, as if each flurry
introduced European cousins or announced
the best feeding grounds for twenty miles and how to fly there
by direct route. Then, suddenly, they're off to their roosts
and the tree
is empty.

We tip up our heads to watch triangular wings
flapping fast,
          swirling small black-feathered bodies
                    into dolphin dives
through the dusk,
          sucking in scatterings
               of flock fragments
like a shaken-out scarf,
          growing wider as it unwinds and flexes.
                    Now there are thousands.

We murmur admiration, imagine ourselves at the centre of this thrilling wave,
warm and safe from predators, soaring at speed in a vast family gathering
high above sheds, reeds, estuary, in a violet-green sheen, slowly darkening.

Out of Sync Haiku

Three nestfuls by May
in one garden shed – each with
five robins. Beaks blunt on hard ground.

If we hadn't helped
to find them worms there wouldn't
have been enough.

So many gaping mouths –
but by July beans ran
green pendants through red berries.

Worms were floating
in our flooded garden, nests void
of beaks lost in soft, grey down.

Summter followed Spwin:
fifteen robins sheltering
in August holly.

Elusive neighbours

There have been no recorded sightings... since the turn
of the Millennium... The cicada emits a high-pitched song
only on sunny days between May and July. So high-pitched...
that it is imperceptible to most humans, especially those over
the age of 40.

Summer sends us on circadian quests to seek them,
these lost cicadas, who have secreted
their highest-of-all song somewhere in this forest –

so high that most humans cannot hear it,
especially those past their fortieth summer –
yet we search clearings listening,

hesitate where bracken seems homeliest
for fertile females, cling to our own twigs
stubbornly, vibrating with sensations –

while their translucent wings swish like skirts
stretched over sparking embers that the sun
refuses to flame to us through their song.

Foxing

I was going to bed when a fox hit my window.
11.30, curtains drawn, book tugging in another direction,
I thought a bird had hit the pane, blown off-course.
That night everything was flying, a spring wind rising –
but a second thump shuddered down the wall
as I pulled back the curtain. A cub fell from the creeper,
sprang to the lawn and fixed me in a defiant gaze.
He backed away, but moments later the window shivered
before he fled, leaving a birds' nest on the grass, no eggs.

My first fox, caught in a cricket net, was a 7 a.m. window-glimpse
of red-brown, flicking more wildly than a cat's tail. One foot hooked,
he thrashed, yelping in panic. The school was shut: I rang the RSPCA.
Eventually, he hung, panting in the new day's heat.
A clamour built up across the field. He cowered, caught out after hours.
A woman with her special crook freed him, checked him out, tied up the nets.
Afterwards, he and I grew an understanding. He would appear on my patio,
safe from whooping cries, and curl up in the sun at my feet,
on the other side of the long window. I liked to think we read together.

I hoped he knew how much I admired his clean dark ears,
his red-gold head and the dark centre of his back – how much
I still felt the hot pain of those hanging hours every time he left me
with halting steps, on his three good legs and the one with a dark tip
that didn't touch the ground. After moving house, I often wondered
if he had survived, if the new owners had made him welcome –
it didn't seem likely. Miles away, missing his company,
I pull down creeper; fix bird boxes high, out of temptation's reach;
wait with my old book for a new visit; notice marks on the page; stroke them.

Between an Old Ash Tree and the Sea

Begun by Gloucestershire rain,
sent south by the force of ice
freshwater meets a North Sea tide
in a seven metre rise
and fall. Wandle, Effra, Roding,
Fleet join Churn, Windrush, Pang, Leach,
Kennet, Loddon, Colne and every
tributary flowing home.

Natives, escapees, invaders –
salmon, trout, tench, bream and eel,
spined sticklebacks, broad-banded perch,
Roman carp, Eurasian ruffe,
barbel skimming the river-bed,
darting dace, slow-cruising chub,
zander, weevers, zebra mussels:
old-timers meet newcomers.

Its source runs dry but the river
flows on: banks burst when rain fails
to cease falling. Upstream, empty
boat-houses beneath willows
pose with coots and grazing cattle.
Downstream quickens; bridges heave
life into the city over
changing water keeping time.

Wolves' Valley

(Wolmecoma, Woolacombe)

Long before Henry dropped hints
heavy as chain mail and the lord from Morthoe
murdered Becket, wolves howled
the sides of this valley, hidden
in its thickly wooded hills. The town where
wolfhounds now watch last surfers
catch waves as light fails, wasn't even
a brief vision in a stroller's eye.

Some men have always lacked balance.
Soon tributes were paid in hundreds
of wolf-skins, woods fired, and men obtained
what they desired by destruction. In that green age
which was our dark time, with eyes
like new moons, wolves padded down
coastal paths long since collapsed,
hunting where trees no longer ruled.

Emerging from a clearing, they raced
along this vast arc of sand, pelts stiff
with salt, their leader looking out
on a bay too cold then for dolphins
or basking sharks, in the days before
long bark-stripped boards
were brought in by waves
not yet created.

And as the pack played
with no thought of the future –
running and rolling, crouching, jaw-hugging –
just as, today, their distant descendants
bark and run at the water – from the corners
of their wolf eyes, seal-skinned men
lifted themselves onto waves in the half-light –
paddling, springing, standing – riding fearlessly in.

Whale Song

Gulpers of light, the oceans you navigate
evolve darkly. You change songs together,
surfacing after each last theme to breathe.
A skirt of sea fills with the same slow shift
of male moans and trills: cold depths cradle
eerie scrapes and groans. Warmth brings confusion.
Like the seasons, we could lose you in this mistiming.

So, let us not be stranded staring
when a young baleen needs helping out of harbour,
or one of her northern cousins can't swing out of an estuary,
though his call is as loud as a jet on take-off
and his four-chambered heart weighs as much as three humans.
Every burning forest misdirects you, disrupts your feeding:
every journey we make now may swallow your song.

Out of Their Element

Heaped by the side of the path
like parts of an old, abandoned machine
or a giant, fossilised flower dusted with lichen,
curved and creased – all that remains
of the Croyde whale, washed up
on the beach in 1915.

The past was this often unnoticed relic or
the whalebone arch in Peckham Park,
passed through by oblivious lovers,
children who'd never seen the sea
and the men who finally demolished it
without a backward glance.

Thirty whales beached in one month this winter,
caught in the maw of the North Sea; lost, hungry,
sonar scuppered by the shallow sandy floor.
Tides licked one afloat before he died. Others
expired beneath bucketfuls of brine, flung to soothe
agony we saw, but didn't see.

Natural Warning, Kaikoura

We can feel safe watching the world's biggest brain,
in the box-head of a deepest-diving whale,
begin to plunge over half a mile, but once
the great tail has tipped and curved with a slow
grace that strokes it gently below a wave
with one last delicate dip and lift, we're left with awe
and a sense of a tenebrous body bearing down
to a squid-filled canyon in a heavy weight of sea.

Glittering eyes loosed the thrill of the hunt when,
casting off from the old whaling station as the wind
started to rise and whistle, the cat smashed through waves
like a jumping jack before its engine cut, to listen
to underwater calls, the boat slowly spinning
in search of a spray flurry, a tell-tale burst of bubbles,
more splutter than spout, the emerging head, a ridge,
the long battle-ship-grey body rolling, sated, to the surface.

Wind from the Antarctic south is 40 knots
but, with his stomach of squid beaks, he seems oblivious
as an albatross arcs between him and the mountains,
so fast, on a gust of storm. He, so slow, flukes flipping
back like another wide wingspan before descending
into darkness. This albatross brings neither gale nor
good winds; like us, he rides whatever current air
or tide offers. Watching, we protect each other.

On land, the unspecified future starts to roll closer,
grow into a wave so big it could wash some of us away.
It's easy to miss the first moment glasses chink
on their own in cupboards, not to register that the floor
is trembling until it rolls underfoot. Then the lamp flickers;
it's impossible to stand. We need to keep our balance, act
before it sounds as if creatures beyond the shelf are calling
in unrecognisable voices, although they have already left.

Over the Top

(for Joanne)

> When you meet someone who you feel
> you have always known – or, at least,
> met before in some unknown past,
> there is a closeness you cannot
> comprehend, even suffering
> caught in a memory, now lost.

We shared the same recurring dream.
Soaked and sliding, we saw the space
to reach before guns took their aim.
We knew we had to run, drop down,
hurl ourselves into the long hole
of rats and mud or we'd be dead.

Born within days of each other,
childhoods hundreds of miles apart,
we experienced those bodies
as ours, yet alien to us,
knew how different they were to
the bodies which we lived in now –

the ones we dressed in women's clothes,
that were clean and dry, kept warm, fed.
We always felt lucky to live
next door, chatted over the fence.
Yet, night after night, she survived:
night after night, I knew I died.

LOOKING BACK

Between four and five o'clock, 10th August 1628, Stockholm Harbour

A hull of a thousand oaks, only four of her ten sails set,
yet a gust of wind bore her down and the *Vasa* sank to the seabed.
No one had wanted to tell the King, who was away from home,
that the men sent to test his fine new ship, crusted with carvings
by German craftsmen, had stopped running along the deck
after only three circuits when it lurched to tip them in the water.

No one had wanted to disappoint crowds cramming the harbour
for the celebrations, or to send their families home, who had
special leave to be aboard. Blindly, they sailed towards five o'clock.
The helmsman, a deck below, could see sky but not where
he was going, felt timbers strain as he leant to pull the whipstaff
and turn *Vasa* into the wind to right her. Canvas cracked above him.

His legs set, heavy with fear. The seaman with the conn was calling
down through the companion, voice warping in panic. The helmsman
gasped up into the small hatchway before its short ladder to the square of sky,
which he could easily have reached, lay down, before sea flooded in
to meet him. He stood his deck, while their shouts and screams flowed
into his lungs. For over three hundred years, mud preserved his courage.

Wandering in the Dark with Mr Dickens

CUSTOMER: Why is this pub called *The Betsey Trotwood* when
it's miles from Kent?
BARMAID: They say she was a local madam – and Dickens lived
nearby so he probably knew her...

Did you, as a midnight flâneur, meet her
on your ramblings when rain-rinsed streets were
sharp with darkened bricks, alleys, uneven stairs –
the other Betsey, who'd just popped out for air
while her girls snatched a fistful of sleep or
led their gentlemen to her battened door?

Did you find her at the refuge with your
lost women, hear their stories, see them claw
at chances (a tablecloth, the household crocks,
someone's watch) before a carriage to the docks
and dispatch to a colony? Did she
add strength to Miss Mary's gentility?

Did rumoured blows, or the handsome young rake
she paid off, inspire her character's new shape?
Did she long for a cottage on a cliff,
want to be a respected, seaside Miss
with only donkeys and pesky boys to try her?
Or was that barmaid another storyteller?

Looking Back

it might seem significant that the holiday cottage
we found for our honeymoon turned out to be little more
than a shed, perilously pitched close to a wild cliff edge –
that wooden walls, buffeted by winds, failed to reassure,
and a week-long storm wrecked what was left of our sleep after
daylight dalliance met evening caresses – that the frantic
scrabbling under the floor brought rats, big as fur hats, diving
into bracken with bacon scraps – that the sea was too rough
to be approached, the jetty, treacherous – that ships went down
and, palms to cliff-face, edging fast as I dared, on a ledge,
breath held, I scratched my bright, new wedding ring, doing my best,
even then, not to look back or down – just to follow you.

Roses from Home

When they walked through the door (straight off the path
into our room), she was carrying roses, carefully wrapped,
stems swaddled in damp wadding. Flushed northern blooms,
their buds just opening in the forward south.

He was not long out of hospital and in pain.
It would be his last journey, but still they came,
my mother driving all the way after raiding precious beds
at dawn. They needed to see where I lived now.

I wonder whether they worried I'd forget them and where
I grew up, being newly married and so far away,
but I think they knew how much I missed home
and carried the scent of it with love.

My father never said much, at least, not to me.
Later, my mother told me how shocked he'd been
by the bare cement floor, one cold water tap, no bath,
a scuttle of mice; how concerned he was at the state of the walls.

The lack of space and heat, coal yard close against
the kitchen window, the want of a back door, he
didn't mention. Nor did she, who had grown up
in a basic miner's home that always had a roaring fire.

They had so little time to spend together
in a marriage shorter than the one I eventually lost.
When I remember the days after they left,
I hear petals dripping gently like ticks of a clock.

Midway Meeting

Between half past three and a quarter to four
the clock face darkened on platform 2
and, looking out, I thought of you, turning
onto the motorway between the hills
already lost to us. As my train started
to pull out and rushed me down a track
of leafless farms – pylons stretching out their arms
to lights in windows (curtains yet undrawn)
casting new pools in muddy yards – towards
a scatter of nearly-Christmas towns, I tried
to follow your spattered lights north, across empty fells,
tried to stay with you driving into the dark.

Dodds Cottage

Condemned more than once,
there had been a time when
you could see through its walls.

Year on year, wattle and daub
were rescued by families of Scutters,
Stevenses, then us.

The dirt floor settled under
foot-wide clay tiles and, later,
layers of lives.

Above a Wiggins-Sankey cistern,
beams bore axe-marks patiently.
Bats left eaves at dusk.

What made it home wasn't
repairs, a new roof,
more rooms, painted walls.

It was affection inspired
in rough-handed men who cared
for what wood and brick became,

who returned to sit in the garden
even when we weren't there,
as an honour, a blessing.

Like the unknown families
who picnicked in our track
on summer afternoons.

Or friends who brought their children
to play in the garden and wander
a lane to the banks of the Pang.

What made it home were neighbours
who dropped in, a milkman who hid
our milk in the bushes to keep it cool,

forgetting to tell us where, and
two black cats, trotting off
across the fields, who curled up

on kitchen chairs before evening dew.
It was friends' laughter, music
filtering through ceiling cracks, the love

in our interwoven lives, freewheeling
as apples rolling together
down our sloping path.

The Choice

I remember a
turning road,
late afternoon but

not yet dusk; the trees
had cut off
life flow to last leaves

and, at the road-side,
a white owl –
wide, far-reaching views.

Life rarely lets you
pause, to choose
to be still, silent

as that nun-like bird
surveying
the world at a bend –

and fear, this brown hare,
doesn't know
where he is going.

Yet darkness holds off,
even so
late in December.

Remember the north
as winter
rolls south and blows you

to the wayside one
afternoon,
so dark you can't see

what lies round the bend
until you
get there. Make a choice:

the steady centre
of the soul,
which still lies between

being together
and alone –
the strength of such poise.

Snowfall

It's strange how little it takes to dismantle a home. The moment
you begin packing – it's gone. You're left with boxes, stacked rooms
that grow colder by the hour – carpetless, curtainless, doors wide-open.
When I looked out into moonlight and stars, the park was filling with igloo-builders,
sliders, sledgers, all grabbing a patch, staking it out. Night froze.
Lop-sided snowmen leaned into the wind or sat lumpily on benches.
I built boxes into igloos, slid through pools on a wood floor,
clambered across my packed-up past. There was nothing to sit on.
I considered the park but it was cold between snowmen. Nothing would thaw.
I was moving house in the snow again, twenty-eight years on, without you.

Now, a different garden fills with blackbirds. Starlings invade without cats to bother
        them.
As another log flares, the moon rises high over oaks through an uncurtained window
and there are stars, like bright snow crystals swirling me back to you for a moment,
to when we were young and searched a moonlit field for two black kittens, whose
        world
became unrecognisable within an hour, as mine was to be, years later. Back then,
they staggered towards us, fur-soaked, hopeful to be gathered up, carried back
in our coats, towards lit windows, where light spilled onto footprints, pawprints,
inextricably entwined, and snow fell quietly, unheeded, between us.

Gifted

The world was yours from the
beginning, but
my father's landlord was

Duke of Northumberland.
Generations
knew land to be rented.

Unlocking a landscape
for me, for love,
took talent; we had time.

You pointed – the top
of a mountain I
didn't know we could climb.

I thought it must belong
to someone. You
convinced me it was ours,

just as you showed me that,
land or water,
boundaries are to cross.

My family rarely
walked together.
After work, my mother

took me to the river
or, in autumn,
to pick blackberries where

a road petered out at
wild Dukes Hagg;
we never wandered far.

You drove to Cumbria,
left the old car
in a track and led me

to a path that vanished
in green. Above,
a dark bulk creased with screes

reared up into the sky.
You didn't see
what you woke in me then,

climbed right past it, but I've
not forgotten
that you gave me mountains.

Legacy

(in memory of Irene and Frank Lomax, for Michael)

We don't know where we'll go when we set off on the journey;
we leave with the tide, trusting it will bring us home.

Remember that we can't always see the birds in winter trees
but a trembling twig sometimes sings.

We keep faith that life will sail through death
though we find ourselves in strange waters.

Remember, we are sea and sky, flowers on the water,
and love in your hearts like hidden birds singing.

HYEM

Hyem

When a place puts its hands round your heart
you feel the gentle grip, experience
an inner lift of spirit, a smile
that claims your face, even when alone.
A sinking sun falling on fields
across the valley, the sense of space
and peace as lives in scattered houses
turn on lights along the river – *hyem*.

Home, where trains ran alongside shipyard cranes
until the morning one of them knocked
our carriage off the line as its jib swung through
the driver's cab. Yet, after the screams,
through shattered glass, voices reassured.
Firemen, who sounded like my dad, lifted us
onto ladders and Scotswood Road soothed
by being dusty and noisy, as it usually was.

When the shipyards closed, cranes were last to go –
sold to India along with the dry dock.
I wondered how they dealt with the shock of heat:
our sky was never the same again.
Yet now, in this southernmost county,
cranes draw me to the water as I drive
down Tebourba Way, hoist my heart high enough
to swing me over the estuary, as if I'm travelling home.

The hearth that warmed the south 'with fire'

England's 'Indies', 'Newcastle is Peru'.
Correct your maps again. Southern flames flare
from gas or wood or disappear like hearths
and northern coal. High-pitched roofs vibrate sun
into more joules of electric power.

Sailing south as far as the mainland goes,
barges of Newcastle coal crept along
the coast to dock, heat steaming pans and boil
white treasure from the sea. Cheshire salt doused
those fires and Newcastle is not Peru.

Yet, from Bolivian mines, forests, fields, they've
come in thousands to call the city home –
from Ireland to India, Pakistan
to Poland, Czech Republic to China
to Bolivia, and from south to north.

In student days, neighbours sold Rama's Ices
from a van, all weather, warmed us with smiles,
shivering at the start of summer. Saris
blew along the street, threading gold between
bright silk before the days of Chinatown.

Older, I'm back from the south, but buses
change routes. A local woman helps, keeping
Eastern Europe in her lilt, yet I would
have missed my stop without a Geordie voice
at my shoulder. He'd noticed and come down

to say, 'Pet, yuh need to get off heor',
with the smile of ancestors from Punjab.
Words that share pitch and rhythm generate
warmth, radiate the generosity
of an inheritor. His voice meant home.

Moving On

In the Haymarket a bus station has been transformed
from cattle crush to airport lounge. I no longer miss
Marlborough Crescent, open to weather. From there, I'd rush
for the trolley bus to school while the abattoir let
blood flow unchecked along the gutter, stinking through fumes
as drivers climbed in their cabs and, one by one, engines
vibrated, buses pulled into stands. I'd leap across,
never connecting that red stream with the death it meant
or managing to link this to cattle sometimes glimpsed.
Our city made blood, tanks and ships. It still stood on coal.

Near to where we waited in the cold, suits with laptops
raise glasses in the lobby of a high-rise hotel.
Phones vibrate silently; clean shoes press the shining floor.
Automatic doors open, close by a subdued road.
Multi-glazed rooms gaze across the river. It must be
better; no more leading to slaughter. Downstream they dredged
the Tyne at Wallsend for the deepest vessel ever
to sail there – fifty feet of it underwater – so
they could load the last remains of shipbuilding up for
Dahbol. Blood down the gutter: water under the bridge.

For the Record

(in memory of Jimmy Forsyth, 1913-2009, 'an honest citizen')

Not quite San Francisco, though Benwell streets rolled steeply down
to Scotswood Road, where forty four pubs wafted warm beer
towards the Tyne. They filled *The Hydraulic Crane, The Blast Furnace,*
The Shipwrights' and *The Mechanics' Arms, The Forge Hammer,*
Miners' Arms and *The Gun* – men like you, Jimmy.
An eye lost 'fitting' in my home town, you used your old folding camera
to distil spirits of faces, lives – the pride a wrecking ball couldn't smash,
which lasts – though a community was scattered, swept into flats
that swayed for years, then fell like those streets you knew so well.

Houses marched down the hill from Roman Fort to armament works.
You watched a tank roll past the *Gloucester Arms* – testing – as the whole street
shuddered, snapped folk in their doorways, waiting to hear when they'd be moved.
They knew the dust on their doors, scrubbed the step to sit on.
Four feet tall, someone's bairn is lost in her new coat, even with a belt,
but she smiles across scuffed shoes and, over there, outside *The Royal Oak*,
an almost-smile under a dark fringe, coat short in the arms, wellied feet to attention.
The photo's for her grandfather who'll soon be blind.

Even the demolition men paid for the prints you took of them. It bought more film
to finish the job. Everyone's here: a window cleaner with his ladders and old cloth,
a butcher with sheets of newspaper by the pigs' trotters, the knife grinder,
lads flashing their new brothel-creepers or leaning against the pawn shop glass,
men waiting for the pub to open, a hoola-hooped lass, Sunday frocks, heaps
of rubble, long gaberdines and wrap-around pinnies. This was your adopted home,
where you lived for years with a tap in the yard, an outside bath, summer or winter –

where you kept a bit of the old bridge on top of your wardrobe, where your pictures
started, on the street corners of a three mile-long road, built for Armstrong
to develop his gun. At the end of every street, a fingered door, stained lino floor,
a fug of smoke where river cold met body warmth and a chinking glass.
When all the streets had gone, soon-shabby sixties pubs, named for nostalgic songs,
drew souls over wasteland below their shifting rooms and you stayed in Elswick

though something had 'gone wrong'. You were robbed, attacked, didn't understand.
Once, you knew neighbours at first-hand but, re-housed in a tower, no one met.
Your friends were on the streets elsewhere, which you walked and worked
to be able to sleep. A community died but – thanks to you, Jimmy –
a record survives as true as you could make it, a fine gathering of lives.

I was a fifties child, born in the hospital on top of the hill, where my mother trained
to be a district nurse. She delivered babies onto clean newsprint many a time,
lost some to poverty – closed a good few eyes. I left home to live in Benwell,
six streets from her lodgings. 1972, still only gas light next door.

Growing up, I'd worn the frocks, scuffed the same sandals, chalked the pavement
for hopscotch, had a spinning top. My Uncle Bob was a dead-ringer
for your chap with a dog, flat cap, knotted scarf – the lot.

When I met you in the eighties, I hadn't seen what you'd achieved –
and you didn't tell me. You talked about why you wouldn't wear your teeth,

about Prudhoe and Scotswood, all those pubs, our shared, loved streets.

Community Nurse

(in memory of my mother, Margaret Bolam)

We preferred not to hear (even anonymously)
details of your cases with our tea, asked you
to lock them in your black bag and district register.
We tolerated streams of patients at the door,
listed messages by the phone: you did the rest –
drove miles through snow and waded up farm lanes
to deliver babies, dashed to bath old men in scattered villages
between clinics and visits to terminal cases – you always coped.

But when you no longer wore the belted blue dress
with its bouncing fobwatch; when a late-night ringing did not lure you
from bed to the empty streets; when, alone, you woke as you chose
to a day in the garden or a visit to friends, I remembered the hectic years –
you, nursing my father until he died, refusing to the last
to let you talk about patients, especially himself. Most of all,
I see you after he had gone, nursing case after case, just like his;
opening and closing the same black bag on your own unprofessional pain.

Cherryburn

(Birthplace of Thomas Bewick, 1752-1828)

Although I never saw her here, a yearning for my mother's voice
draws me through the print room door. This is where she explained
how you engraved, loved to demonstrate the way your presses rolled,
would show the blocks and etching tools, lead them to marvel at your books,
even to imagine you crossing the yard from the old low house
where you'd wake to birds you had inked with care, singing
their hearts out and into yours.
                         Behind this cottage and outbuildings,
across sloping fields, a valley view comes closest to the one
my ancestors would have seen: unspoilt, unbuilt, green –
patched with hedges and fields merging into the Cheviot hills.
As a boy, you made a path to the river, where you plodged past dusk,
parents fearful until your father's whistle lured you home,
your head bursting with creatures, river tricks, the ticking night
of stars. Lady's smocks, bird's-foot trefoil and vetch still grow
by the scrap of sand on the Bywell side, perhaps seeded
from plants you sketched.
                       Then, it was swans, a thrush, woodpeckers, a jay,
the family's cows that you saw every day – or a stag drinking at the water's edge.
Today, across the way from your museum, they're shearing quizzical creatures
with pipe-cleaner necks and fluffed ruffed legs, alpacas-with-attitude,
skittish quadrupeds you might have been amused to etch, but which neither you
nor my mother would have known how to handle.

For What It's Worth

The Quayside is quiet on Monday morning apart from kittiwakes to-ing and fro-ing
from nests stuffed onto ledges or lined diagonally up the Tyne Bridge girders.
Their stink wafts from above our heads as they lift us with their cries – higher than
the upbeat slogans on a nearby underpass, promising that the future is This Way.
Old Newcastle has shrunk, cramped by roads designed to sweep cars
round the city centre, past the Laing and Dog Leap Stairs.

In Eldon Square St George is still slaying the dragon, though
he only managed to defend one side of Georgian houses against
advancing, ill-matched shopping centre walls. From his column,
Earl Grey looks down, hour after hour, on 25 metres of big-screen news.
The Cloth Market is suffering from change of use as we kick through
the butts of clubland, an old café sign etched on Pumphrey's upper window.

No piano or newsreels, but the Film Theatre was saved, and a busker plays
Northumbrian tunes in the Central Arcade, where Dad bought my first EP –
Smetana's *Vltava* – stunned when he discovered how much more it cost than 'pop'.
A hundred and thirty years on, a blue plaque celebrates Swan and the world's
first street to be lit by his incandescent bulbs. It's all snatches of light, from kittiwakes
to – sandwiched between Kwik-fit and the A69 – another bit of Hadrian's Wall.

Sea to Stars

At seven, I rode a piebald pony
on Blackpool sands, the sea
in line with the horizon,
out so far we couldn't hear it
above the jangling harness.

At eight, I groomed Harry Stokoe's horse
inside a cramped shed, dodging
her rheumatic legs. Dinah pulled
a cart of rags and bottles
we'd run out to meet for a few balloons.

At thirteen, my first kiss – from a Welshman
in the Black Mountains – every day
trekking through bracken, cantering
below kestrels. I thought I'd found heaven,
then fell for a boy who didn't like horses.

I wanted him to learn so we could both
take to the downs, but he let me go out
on my own. I tried one last time
but his heart wasn't in it. Much later,
he married a cross-country rider.

Today, on my birthday, I wake to white horses,
sun rising over the sea, and you
kissing the extra year away. We lift
with the light, fall in waves, leave the bed
far below us, riderless, winged.

Soul Mate

We may not always agree on everyday things
yet, fortunately, the unusual doesn't surprise you.
When I said I was taking my mother to Plymouth,
you didn't argue. I wondered if I'd manage it
but she turned up on the train. Later, in a restaurant,
I couldn't hear what she was saying, though she filled
the chair opposite and I found myself smiling
right through the meal. She disappeared at some point
on the way back when I started to let other things take over
but I know she'll come travelling with me again,
whether or not I ask her, and that, when it happens
I'll have someone to tell.

Vera

(December 1924 – February 2010, for Peter)

We knew we'd find her sitting in the usual place,
wearing someone else's hat. Yet she'd greet us
with the same keen, green eyes, chattering
in tongues no pastor would recognise.
We'd moved beyond the despair that swept
across Gunnersbury Park one spring day.
Vera lived in her own home then, still thanking the Lord
as we strolled over the grass, all needing air.

'It's very...', she stared at our sinking shoes
as if they were something she didn't like to eat –
'Onions!' Her laugh lifted us and soon
we were sliding across the wide pan of the park,
through mud, suddenly caramelised with love.
At night she'd wait. 'Do you want to go to bed mum?'
'Not 'arf,' she'd say, but wouldn't know where it was.

Wires were crossed; every gear was reverse.
Following me into the garden, she took a peg and, when
I turned away to the line, planted it carefully.
Weeds were heaped on clean wet clothes, soil scattered –
no point in pointing out the problem. It went beyond
jumping on snails, putting tea bags in the kettle.

A hug, a dance: Vera still laughed,
but soon she forgot, unprompted,
how to get up, walk, sit down –
went into a home, losing her own.
We tried to find good in what was left.

When I took her hand, she'd
grasp it, look into my eyes,
smile, turn to you, the son
whose name burned on her tongue

and, quietly, take
your head in her hands,
stroking it, smiling her love,

wrapping it round your pain
like lint, her hands on your head,

blessing.

Winter Solstice at the High Voltage Laboratory

This big green metallic barn keeps fields in cages –
large ones we could run around in, but never do,
and some so small they sit on a bench with only
a hand entering carefully. At feeding time,
safely outside, keepers switch on the fields, record
how much has been consumed, what damage done, how long
it took. Electrons are excited, and charges,
hungry for volts, grow hot while parts snap or explode.

Now, a shed breaks down – heliotrope above, white
below – like a collapsing mushroom. An ion
engine starts to turn, wind park cables are stressed out,
plasmas used to propel us into space before
the Christmas shutdown. For the year, it's the darkest
day yet, but raw light fizzes in this bloodless zoo
as electric trees wink and insulated seas
flow over the coastline's high voltage silhouette.

Jacob's Ladder

It's not a story in the Bible, a song, or an axis mundi,
but a recurring buzz of travelling light, looping up diverging wires
from a spark, curling indigo-mauve arcs up a straight path until their
trails tail out to bridge the widening gap – and snap before they contact.

It's not a dream or stairway to heaven: those aren't angels ascending
but high voltage wings flexing, rising through ionized air, carrying
a current nowhere. This is how we create – test our connections till
they arc, break – start again with a new spark, sprung from listening in the dark.

Kissing Live

Last night you were suddenly there in my dream
wearing an unfamiliar colour and kissing me in front of my mother,
who asked how I felt about you in a way that told me she already knew
and approved. You didn't seem to see her at all yet she was beside us;
both of you, an electric flux, with me at its heart feeling totally loved.

I grew up used to my head buzzing under power-lines, being unable
to sleep soundly if the flex to a lamp ran beneath the bed
and, aged five, groping in the dark, my fingers tingled in a live socket.
When the shock bit, it lifted me and I thought I'd died – lying quietly
terrified until a pulse throbbed excitement – yet nothing could prepare

for the charge that surged right through my body when you first pressed
yourself against me, and nothing can insulate me now against a lifetime
of longing. In my dream your lips were soft, but the strength behind them
would have flung me through space had you not held me gently, to dip
your face into mine until I forgot what colours were, apart from wonderful.

Lying Fallow

Unweeded, the open plot is dry. Rows
of beanpoles lean abandoned, but the sound
of hidden water
never leaves me.

Birds hop in fruit cages of bleached wood struts;
upturned jamjars topple, and unpruned stems
dangle fat berries
between torn mesh.

I sit facing the hills, sun on my neck.
This is a garden I have come home to:
words grow through silence
or the rustle

of a bird in the bushes, or are found
lying quietly on the page as if
they have dropped gently
out of the sky.

NOTES

Basil Bunting's Shadow (13)
Basil Bunting (1900-85) described writing *Briggflatts* 'in the train on the way to work' (Peter Quartermain and Warren Tallman, 'Basil Bunting Talks about *Briggflatts*' in *Agenda* 16, no.1, 1978, p.16). The *Chronicle* is *The Evening Chronicle*, a newspaper published every evening in Newcastle. Bunting was a sub-editor. He sailed on the south coast for months in 1937 and later studied at nautical school in Newcastle.

    J.M.W. Turner made several sketches of Prudhoe Castle in 1817 and painted a watercolour of it in 1825.

Uisce Beatha (19)
See Seamus Heaney's introduction to his translation of *Beowulf* (Faber, 1999), xxiv-xxv, and his poem, 'The Blackbird of Glanmore', in *District and Circle* (Faber, 2006).

    Uisce Beatha: literally 'water of life', the name for whiskey in Irish Gaelic. The *Sheep Dip* brand of Scotch whisky (minus the 'e') was originally distilled in Scotland for the village of Oldbury in Gloucestershire, where whisky was previously said to have been entered on invoices as 'sheep dip' either to mislead farmers' wives or to avoid taxation.

Solent Song: Thursday 18th September 2014 (20)
This was the day of the Scottish Independence referendum when 55% voted 'no' and 45%, 'yes'. 'Wight Light', 'Wight Sky' and 'Wight Sun' are the names of ferries to the Isle of Wight.

Elusive Neighbours (27)
Epigram: www.countryfile.com/countryside/10-most-endangered-animal-species-britain   The New Forest cicada is number 2.

Between an Old Ash Tree and the Sea (29)
Wandle, Effra, Roding, Fleet, Churn, Windrush, Pang, Leach, Kennet, Loddon and Colne are tributaries of the Thames which flows from its source in Gloucestershire to the North Sea.

Wolves' Valley (30)
Sir William de Tracy of Morthoe, Devon, is notorious for being one of four knights said to have murdered Henry II's former friend, Archbishop Thomas à Becket, in 1170.

Out of Their Element (32)

The whalebone arch walk in Peckham Rye Park, south-east London, was demolished in the 1940s. In January and February 2016, thirty whales died on beaches in Britain, the Netherlands, Germany and France. Thirty three whales died, beached off the coast of Ireland, in November 2010.

Wandering in the Dark with Mr Dickens (37)

It is believed that Dickens based his character, Betsey Trotwood, on Miss Mary Pearson Strong who lived at Broadstairs, Kent.

The hearth that warmed the south 'with fire' (52)

William Camden (1551-1623) in *Britannia* (1586) called Newcastle 'the hearth that warmeth the south parts of this kingdom with fire'. 'England's a perfect world, has Indies, too;/ Correct your maps, Newcastle is Peru!' is found in *News from Newcastle* (1651), attributed by some to John Cleveland (1613-58) and by others to Thomas Winnard.

High-pitched...power: research has shown that the vibrations caused by some frequencies of sound, such as those of higher-pitched music, amplify solar cell output.

Moving On (53)

In April 2009, the last of Swan Hunter's cranes and dry dock left the Tyne for the Bharati shipyard in Dahbol, India's second largest private-sector shipbuilder, ending almost 150 years of shipbuilding by the north-east company.

For the Record (54)

A collection of Jimmy Forsyth's photographs, *Scotswood Road*, was published by Bloodaxe Books in 1986. Tyne & Wear Archives holds over 40,000 of his photographic negatives.

For What It's Worth (58)

Bedřich Smetana's *Vltava*, named after the river that flowed through his native Czechoslovakia, is a symphonic poem from his work, *Má Vlast* ('My Homeland') and was my introduction to classical music.

Joseph Swan (1828-1914) invented the incandescent light bulb, first demonstrated in Newcastle in December 1878. Mosley Street, Newcastle, was the first street in the world to be lit by these electric bulbs.